JUN **2** 4 2016

Behind the Wheel of a
STOCK CAR

BETH BENCE REINKE

The Child's World®
childsworld.com

Published by The Child's World®
1980 Lookout Drive • Mankato, MN 56003-1705
800-599-READ • www.childsworld.com

Acknowledgments
The Child's World®: Mary Berendes, Publishing Director
Red Line Editorial: Design, editorial direction, and production
Photographs ©: David Hahn/Icon Sportswire/AP Images, cover, 1; Glenn
Smith/AP Images, 4; Shutterstock Images, 7; Reinhold Matay/AP Images,
8; Matt Slocum/AP Images, 12; Action Sports Photography/Shutterstock
Images, 15, 18, 20; Scott Scheibelhut/Shutterstock Images, 16

ISBN 9781634074339

LCCN 2015946275

Printed in the United States of America
Mankato, MN
December, 2015
PA02282

Table of
CONTENTS

Chapter 1

IN THE RACE

Zooming around the racetrack, your heart hammers in your chest. You are in second place. But you want to be first! Like your fellow racers, you love to go fast. And your stock car is moving at more than 200 miles per hour (322 km/h).

Up ahead, you see the leader's rear bumper. Can you catch him? You press the gas pedal and the engine roars.

Suddenly, there is gray smoke everywhere. You cannot see past it. But your spotter can. He sees cars skidding sideways on the high side of the track. His voice comes over the radio in your helmet. He tells you to go low on the track to avoid the wreck.

You obey your spotter and drive to the inside edge of the turn. Soon, the air is clear again. With his help, you made it through the smoke without hitting the crashing cars.

◀ Engine problems can cause cars to smoke and make it difficult for other drivers to see.

Your spotter stands high on a rooftop where he can see the whole track. He spots danger and tells you how to escape it. Every driver in the race has a spotter.

The yellow caution flag is waving at the start-finish line. That means racers must go slow because of the wreck on the track. Track workers clean up **debris** from the damaged cars.

During the caution laps, you jerk the wheel back and forth—left, right, left, right. The zigzag motion cleans off dirt and marbles that stick to your tires. These marbles are bits of rubber that come off every car's tires and build up on the track.

Wow, it's hot in the car. Your mouth feels dry. You flip up the visor on your helmet. Steering with your left hand, you grab your drink from the holder. A slurp of the cool liquid through the straw tastes good.

Now the track is cleaned up. It is time to restart the race. You see a flash of green at the start-finish line.

"Green flag is out," your spotter says. "Go, go, go!"

You stomp on the gas and grip the wheel tight. Can you pass the leader and win the race?

When the yellow caution flag waves, drivers must ▶ slow down.

Chapter 2

TAKE A LAP

To fans, it seems like you win or lose all by yourself. But racing is a team sport. Lots of people have worked to help make your stock car a winner.

Months before the race, you walked through your team's race shop. Team members were building your car. Engineers used math and science to design it. Welders built the chassis with tubes of steel. The chassis is the car's frame. It includes the cage that surrounds you during the race. The cage helps keep you safe in case of a crash.

After the frame was built, the car was far from finished. Engine tuners worked on the motor. Mechanics tinkered with other parts. Fabricators bent the metal to cover the car's frame.

A few weeks later, you peeked inside the cockpit of your car. The team had installed a special driver's seat for you. It looked like

◀ Stock car teams work to keep the cars in top shape for every race.

a baby's car seat but bigger. It had been fitted to your body size and height. You climbed in to see how it felt. It was a perfect fit.

After the car was built, the last step was decorating it. The colorful design is called a paint scheme. But there was no paint involved. Your team wrapped the car in giant stickers. Then your car traveled to the track inside an 18-wheel truck, called a hauler.

At the track, NASCAR officials inspected the car. Metal templates fit over the body to check the shape. All cars need to have a specified shape to be legal. Next, inspectors checked the engine, safety belts, and other parts. The officials gave the thumbs-up. Your car passed inspection.

NOT A FAMILY CAR

The first NASCAR drivers raced regular passenger cars. They were the same kind of cars factories had in stock. Race cars are still called stock cars today. But today's stock cars are missing lots of things. There are no horns, headlights, or windshield wipers. There is no trunk and nowhere for passengers to sit. Even the tires are different. They have no grooves. Instead, they are smooth so they grip the track better. Stock cars do not even have doors. Drivers climb in through windows.

Then, it was time for practice. You zipped around the track and got used to its **banking** turns. You and your crew chief talked about the car over the radio. The crew chief is the boss of your team.

"The car is loose," you told him. That meant the back end was sliding around when you drove through turns. The crew chief told your team how to tighten up the car so it would handle better.

After practice, you drove qualifying laps. The fastest car would start the race on the **pole**. The pole is the first starting position.

You mashed the gas pedal to the floor. It felt like you were flying through the turns. Your qualifying lap was second fastest of the 43 cars. Another car got the pole. But you got to start in the second spot.

Chapter 3

BUCKLE UP

Race day began with driver introductions. You smiled and waved to the fans cheering you on. Even from far away, they knew you by the colors of your fire suit. The special suit and shoes protect you from heat in the car.

The crowd quieted as the opening ceremonies began. Your crew stood in a straight line across your pit stall. The stall is like your parking space on pit road.

A singer performed the national anthem. As the song ended, fighter jets flew over the track. The plane engines sounded almost as loud as the stock cars during a race.

Your crewmembers gave one another high fives. Kneeling down, you attached heat shields over your shoes. It gets blazing hot near the pedals from the heat of the engine. The shields keep your heels from getting burned.

◀ Crews often line up in their pit stalls during the national anthem.

You climbed in the window and slid into the driver's seat. Time to buckle up. You fastened the belts of your safety harness and pulled your helmet on. Straps hooked your helmet to your head and neck support device. It is called a HANS device for short.

All the safety gear made you feel like you were wrapped in a cocoon. But it could save your life in a crash.

The steering wheel was lying on the dashboard. You grabbed it and attached it. The removable wheel makes it easier to squeeze in and out of the car.

It gets really hot in the car during races—more than 120 degrees Fahrenheit (49°C). You hooked a hose to the top of your helmet. During the race, it blows chilled air in to keep your head cool.

Your crew chief leaned in the window. He gave you a fist bump. You slipped on your fireproof gloves as he fastened the window net. The strong black mesh would keep your arms inside if the car flipped over.

Finally, a voice came over the loud speaker. It was the command—the moment you and your crew had waited for: "Drivers start your engines!"

You flipped the ignition switch. *Vroom! Vroooooom!* The vibration of the engine rumbled through your body.

▲ Head and neck supports and safety harnesses help keep drivers safe during crashes.

Next, the pace car led the field of 43 onto the track. After a few warm-up laps, the green flag waved. The race was on.

The race would last for more than three hours. But you needed to pay attention every second. Your left foot worked the brake and clutch pedals. Your right foot pressed the gas. Lifting weights at the gym has made your arms and shoulders strong. You can steer the car and shift gears without getting tired.

▲ A pace car leads stock cars onto the track before a race.
The race begins when the pace car leaves the track.

After a while, you made your first pit stop. You needed fuel.
You slowly drove down pit road. A number of other cars also
stopped. To help you find your pit stall, a crewmember held a
long pole over the track. It showed your car's number.

Your crew chief counted down to help you stop inside the pit stall.

"Five, four, three, two, one," he said.

The pit crew sprang into action. In seconds, you pulled away with a full gas tank.

More laps went by. Suddenly you felt a jolt. You had a flat tire. You headed back to pit road for new tires.

The pit crew was fast. But you had fallen behind. Quickly, you got back on track and started passing cars, one by one.

PIT STOP!

Imagine a car getting four new tires and fuel in 12 seconds. That's what happens during a NASCAR pit stop. The pit crew also makes adjustments to help the car handle better. If there is debris stuck to the front grille, they clean it. They might pull a tear-off to help the driver see better. A tear-off is a thin sheet of plastic covering the whole windshield. If the driver needs a new drink, a crewmember hands a bottle through the window.

Chapter 4

THE WINNER IS . . .

Your spotter leads you through the late caution flag. You sit in second position. *Whoosh!* The white flag waves. Only one lap to go. Sweat drips down your face. As you surge forward, your car wiggles. But you hold tight and steer it straight.

You push the gas pedal to the floor. Now you can see the leader's number on his door. On the front straightaway you are nose to nose. You shoot past him for the lead and cross the finish line.

The checkered flag waves overhead. You are the winner!

You let out a victorious yell inside your car. Then, you thank your crew over the radio for their hard work. You could not have won without them.

You turn the car around and drive the wrong way down the frontstretch. You spin the car around in circles to celebrate. You

◄ Winning drivers often drive around the track and wave the checkered flag for the fans.

▲ Many fans stay after the race to watch the awards ceremony.

stop and grab the checkered flag from the flagman. Then you drive to victory lane to celebrate your win.

You shed your helmet and gloves. Your team members gather near the car. Someone hands you a towel. It feels good to wipe the sweat from your face and neck. You take off the steering wheel and toss it on the dashboard.

Grabbing the top of the window frame, you pull yourself up and out. You stand on the car door and throw your arms high in victory. Everyone cheers. Photographers take your picture. Fizzy drink sprays from the bottle in your hand, sprinkling the car and people. Confetti floats all around you.

When you jump down, a reporter holds up a microphone. She asks you questions about the race. Video cameras broadcast your interview to fans watching on television.

Your crew chief grabs you in a big bear hug. Your team owner comes to shake your hand. Your pit crew and spotter arrive to help celebrate, too.

The trophy looks heavy. But you grasp it by the bottom and hold it up over your head. Click, click, go the cameras. When you win a race, you pose for dozens of pictures in victory lane.

Smiling for the camera is easy. The hard part was winning the race. But with your team's help, you did it.

GLOSSARY

banking (BANGK-ing): Banking turns are higher on the outer edge than on the inner edge. Driving on the inner edge of banking turns is fastest.

debris (duh-BREE): Debris is any item on the track that makes racing unsafe. Debris can be trash or a piece of metal from a wrecked car.

frontstretch (FRUNT-strech): The frontstretch is the straight part of the track where the start-finish line is located. The winning driver is the first to cross the start-finish line on the frontstretch.

NASCAR (NAS-kar): NASCAR stands for the National Association for Stock Car Auto Racing. NASCAR makes and enforces the rules for stock car racing.

pace car (PASE kar): The pace car is a passenger car that leads the stock cars during slow laps before the race and during caution flags. Stock cars stay behind the pace car when the yellow flag waves.

pole (PUHL): The pole is the first-place starting position for a race. The driver who wins the pole is called the pole-sitter.

victory lane (VIK-toe-ree LAYN): Victory lane is a fenced-in area where the winning driver and team go to celebrate. Winners get their pictures taken with their trophies in victory lane.

TO LEARN MORE

Books

Filipek, Steele. *Race Car Drivers: Start Your Engines!* New York: Grosset & Dunlap, 2009.

Kelley, K. C. *NASCAR Racing to the Finish.* Pleasantvile, NY: Reader's Digest, 2005.

Roberts, Angela. *NASCAR's Greatest Drivers.* New York: Random House, 2009.

Web Sites

Visit our Web site for links about stock cars:

childsworld.com/links

Note to Parents, Teachers, and Librarians: We routinely verify our Web links to make sure they are safe and active sites. So encourage your readers to check them out!

SELECTED BIBLIOGRAPHY

"Crew Chief Notes: Race Tracks and Pit Roads." *Buildingspeed.org.* National Science Foundation, 6 Oct. 2008. Web. 29 Jun. 2015.

Martin, Mark. *NASCAR for Dummies.* Indianapolis, IN: Wiley Publishing, Inc., 2009.

Norman, Brad. "About Fire Suits, Fuel Cells." *NASCAR.com.* National Association for Stock Car Auto Racing, Inc., 5 Jan. 2015. 29 Jun. 2015.

"The Anatomy of a Pit Stop." *NASCAR.com.* National Association for Stock Car Auto Racing, Inc., 5 Jan. 2015. 29 Jun. 2015.

INDEX

ABOUT THE AUTHOR

Beth Bence Reinke is a health writer, an author of more than a dozen children's books, and a columnist and editor for a NASCAR blog. She is also a registered dietitian with degrees in biology and nutrition.